Lesley Choyce (signature)

The Coastline of Forgetting

The Coastline of Forgetting

Lesley Choyce

Paintings by Judy Brannen

Pottersfield Press

Lawrencetown Beach, Nova Scotia, Canada

Copyright Lesley Choyce 1995

All rights reserved. No part of this book may be reproduced or transmitted in any form or by any means, electronic or mechanical, including photocopying, or by any information storage or retrieval system, without permission in writing from the publisher

Canadian Cataloguing in Publication

Choyce, Lesley, 1951 -

The coastline of forgetting
Poems.
ISBN 0-919001-95-5

I. Title
PS8555.H668C62 1995   C811'.54   C95-950191-6
PR9199.3.C46C62 1995

Pottersfield Press gratefully acknowledges the ongoing support of the Nova Scotia Department of Education Cultural Affairs Division, The Canada Council and The Department of Canadian Heritage.

Book illustrations by Judy Brannen
Cover photography by Lesley Choyce

Pottersfield Press
Lawrencetown Beach
RR 2, Porters Lake
Nova Scotia B0J 2S0

Printed in Canada

For Terry

Contents

11   *Introduction*

I. Currents
19   Lawrencetown River
20   The River Mouth
21   Remembering Summer
23   Lawrencetown Headland
25   The Beach
26   The Beach: Against the Grain
27   Otter on the Highway
28   June 18, Eastward
29   Terminal Beach
31   Half Island Point
32   The Wreck
33   Rocks
34   The Train Tracks
36   The Porcupine
37   A Retreat to Tender Traps

II. The Outer Reaches
43   July 24
44   10 a.m., Graham Head
46   Massey's Beach to Three Fathom Harbour
47   Found Poem
48   11:30 a.m., Three Fathom Harbour
49   The Canal
50   August 5: Three Fathom Harbour
          to Hawkeye Island
52   Wedge Island
54   Facing Rat Rock
57   Retreat From Rat Rock
58   The Riches of Rudey Head
59   Fording a Tidal Stream
60   Return From Rudey Head

III. Safe Harbours

65   August 20: What I'm Doing Here

66   Beach Behind Leslie Island

67   Walking Towards Sellars Head

69   Caprice

70   September 8: The Cove, Seaforth

71   Gaetz Head

73   Rounding Gaetz Head

75   Seaforth Remembered

76   Echinoderm

77   The Back Door of Grand Desert

78   The Chanterelles, The Rage

79   The Range

81   The Chezzetcook Wars

83   Chezzetcook Inlet

87   Epilogue: A Thread To Things

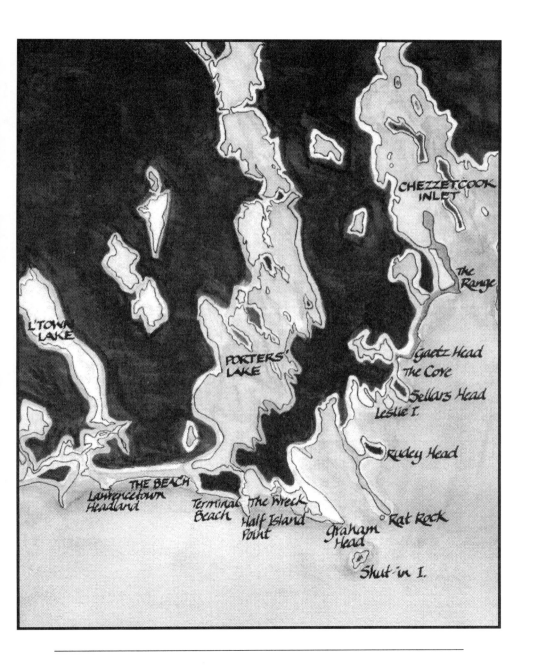

Introduction

The desire to hike this coast was partly a craving to see exactly how it all fit together — ocean, beach, inlet, headland, harbour, swamp, rock reef and sand spit. When you drive on roads, you never fully understand what a land looks like. In Nova Scotia, at least, you only get acquainted with the false perimeter of the life that is tacked along the edge of the asphalt. And along this shore, you can suffer from the delusion that this is a world made up mostly of land — of soil and gravel and rock — when in fact, these are minor components compared to the great over-indulgence of water. From the air, the shards of land here look like something added as an afterthought to break up the monotony of all that sea and lake. The bits of land are, in fact, simply left-overs, the remains of a stubborn glacier's slow retreat.

Very often, Nova Scotians feel like they are a people left over as well, remnants of a grander time. This is, of course, an illusion but the sense pervades the place — once we ruled the seas with our skills at shipbuilding, sailing, fishing and even running illegal rum. Now, old hulls rot at their moorings, small villages are deserted in favour of cities. Whole fishing communities wash away in the newer economics of our times. As a result, places once easy to get to by boat are hard to get to by car. Civilization has retreated inland along much of the Eastern Shore. Paved road frontage, supermarkets, video stores and quick access to the city all seem preferable to a life cohabitating with damp cold salt air and persistent fog. The coast is left to itself and on a few warm summer days, people drive out from Halifax and Dartmouth and are almost surprised to find that Lawrencetown Beach is still there, just like last summer. They might be fooled into believing that it stayed in one place all year. They didn't see it change the way I did over the winter when enormous waves pounded apart the bulkhead and then swept over the road, leaving drifts of sand that eventually blew away in a violent north wind. They didn't see the miles of beaches erode from sand to rocky rubble and back to sand in the space of a winter and a spring.

Not long before I began this hike, I was jolted into realizing how much brutal indifference lurks beneath the ocean's often beautiful exterior. It was the first holiday of summer, and Stoney Beach was packed with swimmers. A mother of four young kids jumped in the ocean and took a step too far out into the current of the Lawrencetown River, emptying itself at low tide into the ocean.

When I arrived on the scene, the sea had already done its work and her body was drifting in toward the headland. I swam out to bring her in but what I carried ashore was not the same woman who had been swept under. It was what is left after all the struggles are over, after the restless currents have changed with the tide. There is a complicated story about what happened after that — the people who gathered on the beach and watched me trying to revive her but refused to help. You've heard it all before. And then there was the unwillingness of men who sit in offices far from the truth of the Atlantic who stubbornly refused to help prevent the next death. There is sometimes a reluctance in government to believe that death is anything but inevitable; it is beyond legal domain.

But an uncaring crowd or a deaf government did not disturb me to my roots as much as the fact that the sea, my sea, had been so indifferently heartless. I had spent considerable time at home in the saltwater, surfing through all the seasons of the year, out past the headlands in Seaforth or beyond the sandy shores of

Lawrencetown or even at Stoney Beach, using the rip of the river itself sometimes to help me get to where I was going. I had surfed the waves from small, generous and forgiving to giant, mean and vengeful, in August and in January. The sea had given me immense happiness and at times unexpected pain. The cold February ocean could be so bitter it would drive like spikes straight into your brain when you went under on a failed attempt to make a wave. I understood the moment of panic when the oxygen is all gone and a frozen, wet darkness is all around, raging like a seismic vortex of seething icy froth, holding you down with its grip.

But the sea had always let go. We had an understanding. And then this betrayal. I wanted to blame it on the government. It was their refusal to provide lifeguards. But ultimately I knew it was not the mere stubbornness of man alone. Still, I returned to the sea to swim, to surf, to walk along the shoreline again and again. I had no choice.

Learning to forget is as important as learning to learn. The Eastern Shore is a place of memory loss. It's a forgotten coast, one of the final stretches of Atlantic coastline to find its way into the twentieth century — and grudgingly at that. The sea forgets its own power here, for in its shroud of fog and cloak of cold it is unaccustomed to swimmers from the cities and knows nothing of the inland hospitality of lakes and streams. And the land, always shrinking back, forgets itself, loses ground, gives way to the sea as it is erased or re-arranged. These thin headlands that arch like fishing hooks out into the sea or the blunt ones that find their bellies carved away year by steady year, are vague memories of the glaciers that abandoned them here. The land forgets itself eventually and becomes sea. The evidence is soon scoured clean.

On the Eastern Shore, the process is relatively rapid. Geological time for this coast is shorter than human lifetimes, sometimes shorter than tenures of presidents or prime ministers. Fox Point and Egg Island were still on the map when I arrived here. The remains of a thriving fishing village still hugged the rocks then and you could drive right out there in a flatbed and haul home

13

the catch. Then the sea grew hungry and soon some teenagers with a few bottles in them went out and torched what was left of the abandoned shacks. Next the sea undid the handiwork of the narrow causeway that leashed it to the land. Now there is little more than a rock reef where waves surge up, collapse, and then spit salt water into the wind.

And at the mouth of the Chezzetcook Inlet was a headland where the military practised dropping bombs, co-operating with the vandal sea until now there remains little more than a scallop of stones sporting barnacles, sea urchins and rusty metal scrap everywhere. John Brannen, a New Brunswicker by birth, who surfs with me on occasion, said of this piece of faulty real estate, "I haven't surfed there since there was a headland." Even the army has abandoned the place since there is not enough land left to make a good target. If the big war comes, perhaps, this could be our salvation: this coast makes a lousy target. The land cannot stay still.

The hike from Lawrencetown River to Chezzetcook Inlet is a record of what still stands and how we who live here are shaped by the sea and by our own forgetfulness. To place foot after foot along this perimeter is to learn a bit more about where I live and who I am. When my wife and I first moved to Nova Scotia, we owned a little house near Chezzetcook Inlet. It was a place of cultivated forgetting for we were from an urban world. Chezzetcook was a place where we untied some of the knots that kept us tethered to cities and failing, dark dreams. The Inlet and its casual drama of tidal changes was a theatre of renewal and reassurance. And now the walk from Lawrencetown to Chezzetcook is an attempt for me to tie back together the entirety of my life along this shore, to lose myself in the forgetful shoreline and rediscover scraps of evidence in the fragments of literature left by man and wave along the coast. As far as I can tell, this is an effort to pin down and record, just once, exactly who I am and where I've been. Then comes the license to sit back and watch the foreground shift with wind and wave until memory itself is a mutable thing like dreams or history or coastlines.

I. Currents

"The sun sings through me. It burns red, a dying ember inside my chest and I am happy to say that this has been my life. Each man must say it to himself: it was mine. I lived it, I was nothing other than what I am. And thankful that it was not a life lived alone. Here on this shore where people try to separate themselves from other living things, I was not among the cursed ones who lived alone. I found and I kept and when time came and tore it away from me, I lingered. I fight and grieve and would gladly tear out the heart of any living god who felt he had the right to claim what was mine."

Jonas MacPherson
The Second Season of Jonas MacPherson

Lawrencetown River

Green fusion, dark in channels,
aches for something broad
but here the river carves the sand,
breeds mussel and crab
and anxious, almost visible swimmers
with lives forever aimed against the current.

A man could never starve here
but could go blind from morning beauty,
go deaf with the quiet
or lose himself beyond repair
in the delicacy of the wind.

Here, fresh water
heaves against the salt,
revises sand into erotic shapes,
with lusty hieroglyphs on the shoreline.
With the proper codebook
I could read these tracks
and other news
left by gulls and herons
at daybreak,
a silent time of light
and longing.

The River Mouth

Driftwood floats in
like the bleached bones of the sea.
The stones own private names
but greet my shoes like old companions.
Like them, my memory was carved
from something hot,
then cooled by time.
The change has made us what we are,
has brought me here to travel,
to remember and to forget.

I'm stalled upon this rubbled shore
where compassion fled from good intents
until my arms were filled
with all the sadness of history.

Here at the headland, things collect
among the rattle of stones.
The drumlin sags toward rockweed fingers
where the river draws out
the warm blood of inland lakes
and cools it with the abrupt patience
of the open sea.

Remembering Summer

And now I'm stopped, I can't move on.
This was the place I tripped to sea
and fell into hostile pools,
stabbed by living blades of whelk and black mussel,
my bones battered by the rocks
until I learned to swim again,
slipping with the diminished current.

Before me I saw the sad, soft shape of a woman's back
as natural as if it belonged here, a creature of the sea —
no human face at first, no panicked cry or signature of fear.
But when turned skyward, the eyes were somewhere else,
some inner harbour, some safer place than this.

No breath, no whisper, no flush of pumping blood,
just cold of white and echoing blue,
the colours the sea would want upon a grave.
She was focused on some farther shore
but I could only turn and swim
back to the one the I knew best,
the waves now helping us in
as the river spent its power beyond the land.

As my feet found the first advancing rock,
I steadied myself,
began to breathe life back into my companion,
suddenly more intimate than any woman
I had ever kissed before.
With each shared breath, the empty eyes
and hollow cheeks seemed more familiar.
I told her I refused to quit
with each new painful breath,
but there was something that I tasted on those lips
unlike any others I had found.

She had no trace of fear;
I had collected it all for myself
and could not hide it as I pushed air into her lungs
suddenly wanting to escape, go home,
and savour the lips of the living.
Instead, blind, sweet terror led me on
as her eyes fixed on that empty sky
and her heart became another cold stone on
this cluttered coast.

When all had failed and a crowd had come,
still white with my first fight with death,
I climbed the cliff,
the hill grown cruel enough
to steal the muscles from my legs
and headed home,
the herons rising up from the marsh
as my throat grew tight
and I wished an end to summer everywhere,
a return to the cold comforts
of the empty shores of winter.

Lawrencetown Headland

There was a church here once
and a post office, too,
high on the green cliffs
with a grand view of heaven and earth.
Both are gone now.
The mail and God have retreated
inland to solid ground
while the sea claws at the roots of land,
giving back daylight to buried stones,
washing away brown mud, like sin,
out to an all-accepting sea.

Up on top, the dirt bikes and trucks
carve ruts like new pews,
as the storms undo the tenuous hills
like a mother unknotting hair.
When saltwater begins to drive the road
the river will chew through from the other side.
Together they will shake off the mainland,
and set a common course toward oblivion.

The Beach

Each seed of sand pulls vision down
until I lose the circus sky
that sings above my head.
I grow vast within each quartzite world
but cautious too and self-possessed
until applause from smashing waves
pulls me back
to the other plane
of distance
and possibility.

I come here often
to see the change of swell
and shift of tide
to mark advances and retreats.
This beach erases the inland ways
and sends me reeling
with mantras of saltwater
singing itself into nothing
on the sand.

The Beach: Against the Grain

Two weeks ago a film crew came
to capture sounds to weld to light.
It took one man to hoist the reel
another just to shove his boom
toward coughing waves beyond the spit.
I waved, advanced and called hello,
one ruined take, another try,
but suddenly the world went mad.
My dog began to bark them back,
my daughter started singing
and anger grew from ruined tapes
until the movie men gave up and left
in search, they said
of sounds more real
more true to life
than all of this.

Otter on the Highway

Just off the beach, beside the marsh,
the neighbour's two red setters
have roused the old otter from the shallow bog,
where she slept as shiny as spilled oil
in the morning sun
believing she was safe among water and weeds.

When the dogs gallop close,
their tongues adrift around their knees,
the otter flees and finds the road,
then struggles west, towards Halifax,
her flippers railed along the yellow line.

A car swerves south to let her pass
and, almost caught by yapping gums,
she dives toward wet freedom at last
while I close my eyes
and hold my breath,
then feel the splash
deep down inside my fur.

June 18, Eastward

Fog begins this leg
but burns to blue
before my feet have found the coast.
The sandpits, round like craters,
undo man's harvest,
reminisce into ponds and gardens
like before.
Out to the rocky shore,
past a beach stone wall,
beyond a desolate post
topped by a rusty basketball hoop
on the landward side.
Then on east, retreating at first
to a field of wild, crawling shrubs —
juniper, just three inches tall
with rooted hands that grip
the mottled rubble of volcanoes.
I slow my pace to smell this breath
of grey-green fruit
while fog falls back from hills above.
I'm alone now
with my wild, brief tundra,
a glacier dump of round, grey rocks
each bold with yellow lichen shirts.
I'm closer now to where I'm from
and loathe to lose what's now undone.

Terminal Beach

The dirt cliffs here
get hit the worst.
I walk the drumlin base
of red mud and spanking sea
and defeated boulders that have toppled down
from the worried hill.
A granite chunk, the size of a pick-up truck
juts out above me
tempting oceans and gravity
against my fate,
for nothing stays the same on this coast
without help.

Farther on, I snake the gulley up
to walk the green, ragged lip,
the cusp of air and continent,
the sea still boiling below,
the mists vaulting up
like liquid smoke.
Each plant is barely rooted here
and some feed down into the earth
so deep,
they break into the sky and suck
the salt this chimney spends.
Like them I know we all might lose
our footing here
when seasons shift
and breach the trust of history.

I poke my stick at horsetail tufts
at moss and tangled weed,
on a wedge of bankrupt land
but then I stop my vandal's act,
for nothing should give up its grip
until the time is right

and I refuse to be the one
to sing the doom of anything
except myself
and that comes last.

For all the fallen work that I've surveyed
I realize now
I've never been around to see
the fall, the sting, the act of end.
Some miracle prevails, I'm sure,
when I explore this tenuous coast:
nothing lets go
till I've moved on.

Half Island Point

The land gives up here all at once —
nothing beyond
but sea and fog and Africa.
At this very, fatal tip, the hill is highest
as if cut off in its ascent
by an envious sea.
Fifteen feet back, just five years safe,
a survey plug of brass
that speaks of men who want to know
how quick the sea will race us home.

Geology's time flies quickly here.
As someone said to me before,
these headlands slip into the tide
before we have a chance to fix
our memory hard on what we'll miss.

And now I'm tacking past the point
of this half island,
walking back toward lower land.
Already these shoes have found the ruts
of four wheel trucks that chase the coast
to look for busted lobster traps
and save the men from staying home
on days too rough to go to work
where angry seas
convulse with waves
and bleed themselves with cold.

The Wreck

The boiler's left and captain's bridge;
he lost her thirty years ago,
the sea grew teeth to chew through steel
and now the bank is littered sheaves
of iron planks and barbs of bolts
sheared down and whittled into bones
of bleeding rust as sharp as pain.

Once violence blends itself to shore,
all broken, useless half-lost things
find refuge here among the rocks,
grow brown with kelp
and red with dulse,
then mussels, Irish moss and snails.

The inlet here is thin and quick
two trimmed spruce sticks
mark fortune's door.
If fishermen from Rocky Run
want home before a setting sun
they have to cut the bargain close
with supper and a tide that slips
to growling rocks
and gruesome chores.

Rocks

All right, stones. Speak.
I've heard you before at sunset
with the waves lancing at the sky
as they smacked you insensible.
I'm not stupid, you know.
Your language is more than
a few hasty metaphors
etched on the broadside of continents.
Fact is, I remember a decade ago
wandering here alone and ecstatic
in the diminuendo of light
and the decline of summer.
I read you like braille
as the tide made a quiet escape
and you spoke outright to the wind
in the compressed syntax of the planet
about the true labour,
of original poets.

The Train Tracks

The trestles lead me
back from the sea
to walk with something set by man,
but now let go —
a place to fish, to dream or fall.
We need to live with hapless things
abandoned when the world moves on.
Forgotten things breed license here —
what man discards might set us free.

A trail cuts deep up into woods
of fern and moss and fallen spruce
with dwarf cornell and chanterelles
and Indian cucumber beneath the foot,
so white and pure down in the soil,
the text says, "spare these rare delights,"
but here the strain grows so profuse
I dig my fingers down to find
this white and perfect part,
a food that tastes of sunlight dreams
and burns all darkness from my heart.

The woods give way to sumptuous marsh,
I use a stick to poke ahead.
Beyond's the road,
another bridge,
the highway twisting off toward town.
The asphalt, stone and paint direct
the lives bent back away from shore
toward steady work and civil deeds.
That selfsame bridge held sway a noose
a young man formed to end his life.
There was no reason offered up
just something
he could never name.

So with my eyes
fixed on my feet
I poke ahead, my stick my guide.
These streams and pools that look so quaint
might yet reveal what I fear most,
forgotten traps for muddled beasts,
and deadly jaws for human meat.

The Porcupine

We meet along this inlet shore
of trees and stone, each backs away,
both blind and fearing shadowed facts,
both prone to break the other's trust.

Your needled fur, like missiles cocked
but I'll avoid those deadly tips.
You take your time in giving up
some morning feast that I can't see
but soon your startled hide retracts,
you waddle off toward mystery.

And when I look to see your meal,
there's nothing but a plastic jug
all chewed and chipped,
a moron's feast.
What drove you to this fool's repast?
Or is it just that each of us
must gnaw away at all that's tossed
from other worlds less understood
until our quills grow blunt and dull
and poison tastes like something sweet.

A Retreat to Tender Traps

Near the mouth of Rocky Run —
a fragile channel and a long spit of shaggy rock
still bar me from the open sea.
I feel inland and cheated,
too late for missed chances to ford the shallows
so it's back toward land
still needing first to catch the sting of icy streams
until I find I'm into muck beyond my knees
and reaching up with hungry gums.

I'm free at length and doubled back
around the snake, I'm barefoot now
and fighting for my space
on crowded floors of living shells with razored beaks.
Another try, it's quicksand now, of sorts,
and oh those happy clams
who sense me sinking in the soup —
an old relation coming home
but finally a place is found,
a plane of corrugated sand
and I discover my feet upon
God's own, uncharted clam bed,
untouched by all the diggers of this world.

But now the sky grows wild with living wind
and dancing birds who want this place;
I'm crowded now by dowitchers and siren snipes
all needle-nosed and locomotive-legged
who flutter at my advance
until I crawl way up, above the bar
to beachrock and glasswort
and an infinity of spider legs.

My hand moves to shuffle the stones
and write among these rocks

of all the miracles
just as a lone sparrow
attaches itself to a swaying stem of sea oats
beside my cheek.
The wind begins to dry my feet,
the sun pretends it was
and will forever be
like this eternal present
flashing phosphorus
on the landscape of empty history.

II. The Outer Reaches

"Just then the waves began to lap against my shoes. And when I looked at the sea, I saw that the water looked like it had been sprinkled with green and silver jewellery. A war had broken out somewhere on the planet, but it wouldn't reach us here. Pieces of the world's crisis would wash ashore and remind us all of the turmoil elsewhere, but we would live long and free in the Republic of Nothing and when we died and our souls became as light as feathers, we would dive straight into the sunrise and ride the backs of living elephants."

Ian MacQuade
The Republic of Nothing

July 24

After three near drownings again
at the beach that began this search,
a cold, hard fog set down and clamped us close inside
but now the sun has torched her ropes
and opens the cage that ruled my heart.

Picked up the trail at Rocky Run wharf
empty like an unbought post card.
I duck under a half-built pier further up,
can't see the man but his hammer knocks
hard against the blue morning.
Looking up to find the source,
I'm staring into the eyes
of a black ceramic boy with a fishing pole
who finds me such a curious catch
left over by the tide
that his grin goes ear to ear and back
but I slip on beneath him, afraid to meet the hammer hand
of the wharfman who owns this place.

The stoney shoreline is anchored to earth
by snails and dark periwinkles;
they suck these rocks
and breed in tide-abandoned pools of brine.
Their stomach-foot slips in and out
while I try to dance around them, mostly in vain
no virgin stones are left unridden
but if I lower a hand to scoop the snails
they shrink inside and close the door
and let me toss them out to sea.
Despite their size and carefree minds,
these meek have owned this coast so long,
that when my feet are gone, they'll have it back;
when men are gone,
they'll own it more.

10 a.m., Graham Head

My heart still pounds
hiking up this headland,
this last landward point twinned with towers
built by Navy men, ventriloquists who wish
to throw their voice to sea.
Before me now, Shut-In Island,
a barren place of gull and crag
surrounded by an armada of seals
and home to shipwrecked souls.

Spruce jungle gives way
to blueberry, cinquefoil
and pungent herbal growth.
Here at the top I see
my first clear view of Chezzetcook,
its wide mouth grinning at the sky
but between us yet,
the crooked back of Hawkeye Island,
Wedge Island and Rat Rock.
Each must be met before my end.

Barbed wire lies lending its colour to the grass,
grey delicate fungus
like ornate earrings
dangle from each red knot of iron
that blooms like an angry flower.
Still troubled on this promontory
with my fight with government.
Can't quite free the grip of battles lost.
I look back beyond Terminal Beach
to Lawrencetown, still there,
now seeming far inland and safe.
But there's more safety here, I know,
at the trace root of the land's bulging memory,
garnished with shriek of gull

and burnished coltsfoot.
A blue iris blooms
upon a shred of turf
with empty air beneath its roots.

This dirt cliff, too,
will soon forget
that I was here.
My footprints soon
will wash to sea
as soil slips free
its compact form,
takes flight,
and empties all it knows.

Massey's Beach to Three Fathom Harbour

From the headland, a scree jump
down half the mountain
sinking in mud soft as sentiment
then tobogganning on shale
to the stony base.

A mile or so on loose rock,
each step undoes the law that rules here,
echoes against the high shore
like Nazi jackboots in a foreign film.
But I'm alone here,
my own political act,
a fascist only
in my desire
to impose my will
upon myself.

Along the eastward shore,
all flotsam and boulders
whitewashed by gulls,
noon arrives above.
My feet turn rebel,
want something flat and paved,
but up ahead, acres of mud and sea oat stubble,
beyond a canal that failed to tether
Porter's Lake to the sea.

Found Poem

Sea rocket, rockweed, crab shell, razor clam
Orach, lichen, mussel snout, algae
Eel grass, lobster pot, driftwood, herring gull
Warm stone, cold stone, every stone the sea gave back.

I stop to fix on what I am:
Backpack, shoes, fingers, ink,
Something moving upon a page.

11:30 a.m., Three Fathom Harbour

Clam beds now — soft, footsucking mud
and vivid streamlets running south.
The harbour will be full up soon
to end decisions about where to walk.
I hope to beat the tide
and sprint
across a patio of slime
skinned over with a crust
of sun-fried eelgrass.

Speed, I decide, makes a lighter soul
so I charge across
only to find my self half way
up to my crotch in silt
and staring down an awkward death,
mud already grabbing
at what's left of my manhood.

I heave my pack to higher ground
and lean as best I can,
to swim perhaps, or crawl or flail
as I watch my skin begin to turn
its way back into the ooze.

But one foot has found its freedom
even as it clings in communion
with who knows what
sort of worm in these depths.
In a fresh advance, I ascend from muck
evolve back to a man,
my gills closing tight as I nurse my pride
and rest beside
a tin cup with buckshot holes
cradling snails and snails
and more snails.

The Canal

Tide driven into the trees
I wring my socks and harvest the shade
but already the mosquitoes, the blackflies
align in armies against me
and drive me back to the shore
where deertrack leads through grasses
that slide their razor edges along my shins
leaving the foam of spittle bugs
like white frothy moons
clinging to my kneecaps.

The canal from harbour to lake
is shallow here.
Once dug from rock with steam machines
that gorged out shale and slate,
it's now a half-failed stream
with beards of trailing algae,
unsure at times which way to flow
with tides that pull from either end.

When I reach the road
some tourists have stopped
to lean the bridge rail, and discover what?
A wild man emerging from the bush
to shock them back into their Ohio selves.
They spill what's left of their styrofoam coffee
and fold themselves back into their car.

I feel guilty now
for they were so absorbed in the sight
of the unkempt marsh
that my arrival denied their discovery,
made them remember that man
must have his small dominion
in whatever way he can.

August 5: Three Fathom Harbour to Hawkeye Island

Begin at the clam beds, half asleep,
this time my brother is with me,
the road has led him here.
I think I want the clear blue harbour and roofless sky
to burn us back to boyhood,
a chance to talk, without TV or families,
about our unfamiliar selves
while dancing on the rounder rocks
and waltzing towards the sea.

There's always the excitement to push
on to find the farthest point
of any headland
and hike up into the grassy heights
and see how severe the land is cropped.

We have forgotten we were brothers —
old arguers of pointless truths,
fighters at suppertime
and victims of the same discipline.
Almost none of this is carried
in the rucksacks of our memory.
Now he has two sons
who drive the light from the sky
with restless child ambition
and I have loosed two daughters
who see beyond all my own striving.

A causeway tethers Hawkeye Island to safer shores
and brings us to the fishing village,
a colony of perch-grey cabins
and gravity ravaged wharves
that sink themselves into the stuttering sea.
A rusting school bus here sits squat and severe
convinced at last by salty air

that it is nothing more than wreckage,
no longer worthy as a fisherman's shed.

Our feet stir stones from the cobbled road
and send grasshoppers stinging the air,
snapped loose from drying beach peas.
On a bludgeoned stage, one man at work:
Joe, who sells me cod for a dollar a throw,
him with a mangled hand, a lobster's claw.
He lost spare fingers once in a stubborn winch
and saw them tossed into trawler tubs,
with other fish for freezing.

When he sells me a fish, he jigs the knife
up once and out and slops the hulk
through a three-month old bath
of rain and slime and fish scales
and drops it in a Sobey's bag
then slides the dollar from my grip.

Now Gordy and I have left the wharves,
begun the tricky jetty walk
on hopeful rocks that link (in theory)
Hawkeye Island to the Wedge,
a wounded blade of pummelled hill that's lost desire
to fight the storms.
The tide sneaks up
and we'll have to scramble
to make it there and back.
The wind has found us too
and waves will want us wet
before we're through.
Already spray shoots overhead
and lets us lick the salt
like pungent childhood tears
that travelled ancient routes
from eye to mouth.

Wedge Island

We walk the Wedge from inner tip,
a well-honed ridge of clay and rock
forgetting that it once was fat
and trussed a mighty headland
to the coast.
This acid sea again, at work,
in patient mutilation,
erasing, removing,
denying memory.

I remember a hike here once,
midstorm,
when seas rifled reports
and lemons bobbed around the foam,
a crate of yellow balls
loosed from some distant ship
for the waves to juggle
then toss toward shore.
I tasted one; it stung of sour
and salt and something else
not right for shores this far up north.

The gulls control this place
as the narrow splays out
into a broad green table top.
They gather by the hundreds
to eddy about — loud, threatening,
for we have arrived at their resting ground.
They shriek and dive
and carve long shadows with their wings
as they fence us in with their fury
and stage a frenzied ceiling
hung low beneath the clouds.

We meet one young, pedestrian gull,
then two,
both grey and downy
and confused by our shape.
Dead brothers and sisters appear,
caught in low alders,
picked clean by cruel relations
with careless hunger
and sharpened beaks.

Facing Rat Rock

The tide has sealed us off
from one farther island,
a low lump of stone
whose name seals its fate.
A gutted shack stands above the rockweed
and we think that would be a good place
to undo
whatever ties a man to civilization.

Clear pools grow red and golden fronds
and periwinkle shells make minarets along the shore
where a thousand snails have crawled
to issue up these bleached monuments
before drying up to death
beneath a helpful sun.

The sea does here
what must be done,
carving away at things that are hard,
stealing the soil and littering rocks,
then giving back new life
to glisten like jewelry
that sits out high tide before slipping home.

I ask my brother what things make him happy
but he doesn't know.
We share an affliction
with much of the world
and the more I pry
at what makes him tick,
the more we confound ourselves,
give up, leave the logic to the mounting wind
and screaming gulls.

High up on the Wedge Island top
we find a well —
the walls of the ridge drop off close on either side
but when we lift the cover
the water sits high;
it's fresh, not salt, and nearly spills above the lip.
With opportunity still alive
we close the lid
and leave the fount untasted.
There's something to be feared perhaps
from water trapped like this
and surrounded mostly by sky.
My brother is thinking of bacteria.
I'm wondering who tapped this hill and when
and what of the powers of something wet
that pushes up
from such dark stone depths?

One day soon, the sea will meet this well
and steal the rocks that once made walls
until it gushes free on every side
and spends itself at last
in salt.

Later,
I recognize what we've missed:
a chance to taste of something pure.
We've backed away from cliffs again
and scatter all the fledgling gulls
who make for flight
but fail to rise
as elder claws flash past our heads
and wings flap hard
like circus tents about to fall.

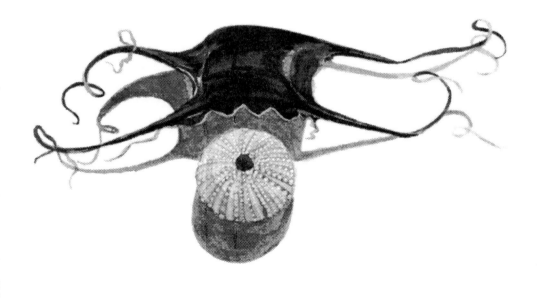

Retreat From Rat Rock

Hunkered down behind jagged rock
a cabin sits,
well kept, correct,
a tiny patch of lawn
on soil as thin as a spinnaker skirt —
some thesis of order here
set against all the will of chaos.
Nearby an outhouse fades to grey
against a lichen-bright molar of granite,
a backdrop of igneous and stubborn life.

The gulls give way
to manmade and unmade things
as we trace the east cliff down
to the ribbon of cranky rocks,
then dance them north from splash to splash
along this backbone
built by men
who could not quite
let the Rat, the Wedge
go free.

The leash, we know, will not last long
and soon the stones will tumble down
in boiling seas and subtle storms
designed, no doubt, to undermine
all the politics of permanence.

The Riches of Rudey Head

A thread of rock and drift
across a lazy inlet
tethers what should be an island.
The land forgets
but it doesn't always want
to let go.

Along the strand my brother finds
square gold
buried like teeth in larger stones
and I refuse, at first, to tell
the truth of pyrites.
Our genealogy is studded with golden cubes
that blaze like burning eyes
from boring stones.

But this was never a prosperous shore;
we settle
for the gold of fools
anywhere, here
along the shore
of Rudey Head.

To tease the air,
I spill the truth
while poised on a giddy log.
But my brother will carry the find
a long way home,
believing, no doubt, I'm wrong,
aware of my long history of mistakes
and never fully trusting me
to judge the worth
of vital things.

Fording a Tidal Stream

We take off shoes,
to forge across a thin, deep creek.
I take off my pants, a pioneer;
my brother roles his cuffs to crotch
to chance the growing tide,
a stranglehold of cold
wrestling against our legs.
I welcome pain because, at least,
I know I'm full alive;
I'd want for nothing less.
A land of perfect beauty
must greet its customers
with knives of cold
that thrill the blood
and skin the hide of dullness
from all biography.

Return From Rudey Head

We have walked our wings to dust
and found a way back to safe origins,
calm mud, salt flats, a paved road
heading inland.
My brother is still confused, I think,
by the purpose of what we did.
A practical man, he works for pay
and never grew to trust
the link of leisure to profit.
I'm mending nets, I explain,
these shards of land,
these bays and seas, I weave
it all inside my mind.
Nothing slips past
before it's caught and studied.

The trick, I tell him,
is just to let things go
before they die,
to capture, release,
capture, release,
then make repairs
on the homeward leg.

III. Safe Harbours

"There was a time of dark which is always a time of difficult decisions. The dark contains infinite possibility. It is a time when dreamers do not wish to awake. There are so many decisions to be made if one wants to create from the dark. First there is a selection of form. Many desire to be the white soaring birds. Some collect the darkness into the shape of wings and grow weightless, rising into the light, then spiralling down the invisible inverse tornado, descending back into the world.

Many are so seduced by their new form that they will never go back to being bound to the earth, back to being human. Others feel the fluid movement of the dark and want a life in the sea, never touching the shoreline at all. Then one becomes a dolphin or a whale. Many return quickly, released by a harpoon or a hungry shark, saying that the pace was too slow. A few linger on for generations in the deep, always returning to the dark with a brooding temperament but an understanding of the aqua-earthly world that fairly quakes inside them like a great river."

Obsidian
The Trap Door To Heaven

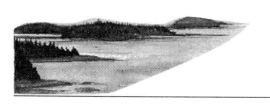

August 20: What I'm Doing Here

A hurricane is out there today
wanting to get ashore —
Alone again, I push the warm wind east
and breathe back into that heavy breath
of a summer sea
and another ending season.

What I'm doing here
is an act of margins, a fight
against old age, finality.
My mind is filled with checklists
for this life and the next
but this walking along
the coastline of forgetting
cannot wait.
When I return next time, as a porcupine
or a pigeon
or a stumbling Halifax bum
these stones will have shrunken back
towards Truro
and the evidence will all be drowned.

Beach Behind Leslie Island

The sky is grey —
thunder now and a ragged sea.
The peace of this inner beach
and a pond filled with a ballet of rockweed
is a short reprieve
from the pace of measured life.
I collect this speck of time
like a dark, polished grain of sand
and stash it in my head
to see how long it takes
to leak back out
and leave me anchored again
on a stoney beach
of another tense tomorrow.

Walking Towards Sellars Head

A grey sky suggests the infinite.
Add pebbled beach and thin, insistent waves
and footsteps
shuffling toward the moon.
The spruce don't know me here,
stand back from the tide
and ram the low sky
but along the way, one has fallen
into some forgotten higher tide.

We have all been fooled by these stones,
poised like miracles at the break
but once pocketed and dry
they turn brown to something
less interesting than dust.
And distance sneaks its way home here
from short to long
to receding headlands and landmarks
that wander at your approach.

At last I catch up to Sellars Head,
this mottled remains of land's memory
knocked by windy seas into a pile
of broken teeth and greenish foam.
A thing like me is of little interest here
to the assembly of empty spaces.
From a slippery toehold
on the temple of Sellars Head
I peer down to the greedy fingers of kelp
twirling circles around the roots
of sunken trees,
then climb below and test the current.

When the herring gull dives
to his favoured pool,
he finds the rocks have come alive,
grown legs and arms
and eyes of endless wonder.

Caprice

This week,
the Tropics turn
and venture north
to rush this coast with seas of thunder.
I'm tired too of a docile summer;
let heat avenge us with murder
before we step back into winter next.
Even now, as the Arctic inhales deep,
ready to blow the ice back into our veins,
the South Atlantic is on the make.

Tomorrow when the waves explode
along this bouldered point
I'll stroke the sea to prove my dance
upon their backs
and carve my name on ocean walls
then drive for frantic light
as they tunnel on the reef
and I pretend I know their ways;
I've walked on water all my life.

September 8: The Cove, Seaforth

The railroad is erasing itself.
All summer, men
with rust-stained skins
have undone ribs of steel
that linked this shore.
The owners want it all away —
the gypsum's gone for good.
These Seaforth rails will melt
then boil
and pour themselves in something else
until this spur
is everywhere but here
where wave roar and diesel thrust
once staged a volley of staggering noise.

Here at the cove old boxcars
once lingered a winter;
the freight men hoped they'd just disappear.
The sea and other vandals
would be a cheap wrecking crew
but never quite up to the conspiracy
of shaving six inch steel
into blossoms of rust and thin air
in a single season.

In fifty years the rail has been and gone.
There's nothing left but me
on foot above the tide
collecting wasted bolts as red as dulse
and heavy as the anchors
of unwanted history.

Gaetz Head

An old stuffed chair
sits snug at the foot
of a sagging mudface
flush against the sea.
Washed in, it waits
for the living or the drowned
to rest here between the day's hauntings.

The brown plaid bulwark,
soaked to the springs,
and sprouting coltsfoot from the arms
has stoppered a deepening ravine,
clots up from behind with red mud
and quartzite,
a parlour of debris.
I think of love,
of noble, failed attempts
to hold what was already lost,
of elemental forces that set me
to shore-up weak headlands
with the mouldering furniture
of half-lived dreams.

I think of how we always
lose grip from the roots
but on the surface never give,
sustained by the arrival of living things
that grope for light in short seasons
along dangerous perimeters.

Rounding Gaetz Head

If these are heads
then this province is a medusa:
where the sea chops one off,
ten more appear.

Coltsfoot and sofas
of washed-in kelp and rockweed, angel hair and dulse,
I walk across a spongy path
and go dizzy tracing with my eye
the footpaths of spiders
who orbit stones
and ricochet from slate to light.

When I pound my feet
across the clatter of these rocks
I believe that this is a better life;
I'll never return to housebound daydreams.
The blood moves quicker here from heart to head
and Seaforth shores correct the tides inside my veins.

I splice my route through mud-stained stones
and green grass chewed
within a tooth of earth
by bright-eyed cows with whipping tails
and tags on ears that date soon death.
The cows alone bear witness here
except for sparse and purple bolts
of nettle and bright bull thistle.

Up ahead someone has fixed
a Red Sox cap to a bleached cow skull
that smiles back to its barn
with all its teeth intact.
Here's a place of sacrifice
where flesh is left for scrounging gulls

and low-tide crabs who lie in wait for rotten meat.
It's the price that's paid for a well-fed life
and a safe career behind a fence.

My feet have quit, I need to move.
If an east wind grows and finds me here
he'll chase the proper tenants out
and teach me how to spiral up
into a brackish log
and soon forget what brought me here
and made me real.

Instead, I'll anchor back
into the urgency of algae
swarming in the shallows:
the rent is due
and the mind is clear.

Seaforth Remembered

September and the geese
flap past this cliff,
like a knuckle bent against the sky.
Across the road, a man still dips
a bucket from a stoned-in well
and there beside the thin, steep church
my wife and I once lived.
We'd just come north, like refugees
and Seaforth helped to clean our wounds.

Cormorants,
their wills gone weak,
are fleeing south
at the first mild frost.
We almost quit this country too
but grew too fond of a clean, hard land
and lives that fit like favoured dreams.

Echinoderm

The tide runs desperately high
lapping up the land
reminding me of a flood of years
full of things
so important
I used to wake up at nights
sweating blood and laughter
through my dreams.

At night, the moon drapes the land
with borrowed light;
the sea absolves itself
of a six hour prowess,
retreats grumbling.

As I walk, I'll scavenge the beach
for gifts from the night:
for rootless kelp, for gutless fish,
for the remains of creatures
who wear their skeletons
on the outside.

The Back Door of Grand Desert

Forded a brook that sips the tidal lake
through dunes of soft white glass.
The headlands are all behind me now,
backed by a dark nimbus sky.
Spruce trees wall the lake
while dry bones
lounge on sandy shores
waiting for storms
to float them to heaven.

I'm near the end but stumble on —
the haunting truth, I'm nowhere near.
The coast goes on and on and on.
Its million miles will call my bluff,
remind me I know nothing yet.

The sun stains the other side
of the inlet now,
I see the other shore.
With a narrow blade of copper light
I see the green crown of the eastern side.

The farther shore reminds me this:
if I were free to circle round
the entire length
of the continent's coast
I'd end back here, a stranger still.
I could not come back to tie the knot
of ending to beginning
since change still rules this ragged edge
and sets my seasons singing.

The Chanterelles, The Rage

A field creeps down to the edge
in wild aster and goldenrod,
a seduction of inland ways,
and I'm drawn up to the higher land
then pulled inside the woods
by colour on the needled floor.
Mushrooms — this year a bumper crop
from endless rains and cold
(our summer spent itself in two weeks,
a heartless thanks for surviving winter).

This duel I've staged with death is here again.
The glowing amanita I can trust, it's poison worn
like a harlequin shirt
but the chanterelles (their very name a song)
are dull gold gone ripe
and mostly safe but some are not.

A mushroom calls you down
beneath wet blue-green boughs
to judge the dark regimes.
The forest draws me further in
then sets me down to teach me this:
false chanterelle (the poison one)
has blades for gills beneath the cap;
the real one's blunt and small
and underneath, the ridges bridge
like nerves or veins inside your wrist.

The Range

The Range
is off-limits.
The army used to practice here
with bombs
until the headland was gone
(they blamed it on the sea).
They've left this land alone now
but still try to keep us out.

On either end is a strangled fence
with posts uprooted like carrots
pulled from sandy soil.
Each month a bulldozer comes
to heave up new impediments
but the young men of Grand Desert
come back at night
to liberate this land
for motorbike and four-wheel truck
and all the restless pursuits
of destructive youth.

The danger signs are riddled with buckshot
and their warning of unexploded bombs
is read only by the sky.
Coastal folk never give up beachland to anyone —
military or rich Americans.
They keep coming back
for sand and gravel
and anything the sea gives up.

I remember surfing here once
when the bombs still fell.
An old B52 was diving toward the sea,
and puffs of sand blossomed on the beach
like flour sacks

tossed to a starving desert.
But something caught above
and failed to fall
then made its drop into the waves
so close it caught me with its splash
but nothing blew
and I was safe enough
to shake an angry fist
at the noisy sky.

The Chezzetcook Wars

This final decimated headland,
the last limping leg of my hike
is littered with jags of bombs,
incendiary metal shrieked and torn
into (almost lovely) rusty flowers
that bloom like peace along the shore.

I study each step and think of other soldiers
marching mined highways,
feeling good about each suck of air,
gripping it in the lungs against the chance
that each step, each breath, might be the last.

I flinch back from a bruised metal can
straight in my path
only to see that it's an empty Keith's
with a defeated label.
A horsehead seal
four yards off shore,
wonders why I'm here.
Beneath him, the sea must be
a corrupted archives
of practiced wars.

Old cars have found their way here
to die among cousin wreckage:
barbed wire coils and cracked wood stoves.
This graveyard of metal
must suit the hungry sea
whose salt undoes the scheme
of our own ruin.

The inlet, a languid blue,
bobs two fishing boats wanting land.
Years ago I took my wife and brother

across the wide channel here —
a rubber boat bucking a clever tide
that begged us out to sea.
My brother and I worked hard as hounds
to make the other side
then laughed at our good luck
only to struggle worse
on the west return
with a rip in the boat
and gulls of fear
circling high inside our hearts.

Chezzetcook Inlet

I end here, a safe harbour,
calm waters studded with leftovers
of danger and risk.
Chezzetcook Inlet —
it sneaks up to the hills
and sprawls over wide clam flats
with half-drowned oval islands,
converting land to sea and back again
with each tidal sweep and timed retreat.

Beyond the bombing range,
still haunted by the junk of war
in such a place as this,
I think of Lebanon, Iraq or worse.
I feel the anxious grip of fear and hate
from each metal blossom
like funeral flowers reminding me
of my own lost battle
to save the woman of Stoney Beach.
How can the sea remain
both death and life for me,
an ally and an enemy?

This Chezzetcook, this plain of blue and green
is what I found fifteen years ago,
marvelling at the sanity of this place
and wanting to settle here
to allow the mind some time
to let the land and sea inside.

Having hiked each step
of this private shore
I've drawn a net around those years
and pulled it tight
around my feet.

I feel like a blind man
who has just felt each wrinkle of his own face
for the first time.

Up ahead my wife waits
on a softscaped beach
with sandwiches and love.
She folds my world into herself at night
and while we sleep I fancy back on who I am:
this place, this coast, this sea of flux,
this perfect map of change
that forgets the names of man.

Epilogue: A Thread to Things

There is a thread to things that keeps us linked,
and pulls me to some perfect past
where loose ends gather
knots of love
that anchor truths
of now and then.

I'm stitched to things that keep me whole,
my fingers make them mine,
but only since I give them back
to other workers on this seam,
the joining grip,
the needle's point,
the always empty I.

My back is bared to earth and rock,
the flesh beneath this vest
and all my arms are stretched like thread
around what I love best.

There is a thread to things that makes us bleed
when pulled too tight,
too much to match
some ceremony's stiffer wrists,
some scoffer's throaty laugh.

We've pulled the length,
now let it go;
it runs its course alone.
For everything I've now become
I owe more than I own.

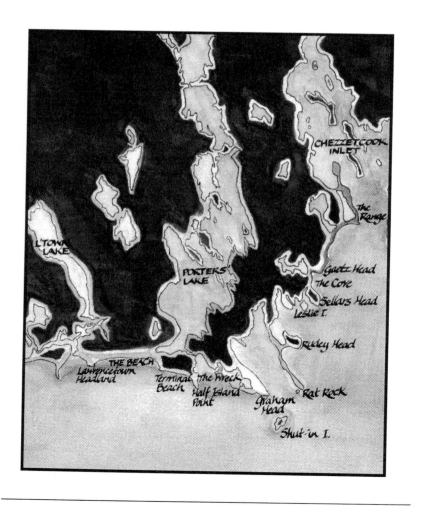

Lesley Choyce lives at Lawrencetown Beach on the Eastern Shore of Nova Scotia. His recent novel, **The Republic of Nothing,** won the Dartmouth Book Award.

Judy Brannen is an artist living in West Chezzetcook, Nova Scotia. She and her husband, John, are leather craft workers and run a craft shop called Laughleton on the Shore Road.